UoLearn
Easy 4 me 2 learn

Developing Your Influencing Skills
A guide to developing the 7 traits of influential people
Lois Burton and Deborah Dalley
Skills Training Course
www.UoLearn.com

Also by Deborah Dalley : Developing your Influencing Skills,
ISBN 978-1-84937-004-2

Successful Business Writing
How to write excellent and persuasive communications
UK spelling version
Heather Baker
Skills Training Course
www.UoLearn.com

Practical and Effective Performance Management
How excellent leaders manage their staff and teams for top performance.
Lots of exercises and free downloadable workbook.
Steve Walker
Skills Training Course
www.UoLearn.com

Report Writing Skills Training Course
How to write a report and executive summary and plan, design and present your report.
Dr Margaret Greenhall
Skills Training Course
www.UoLearn.com

Stress Management Skills Training Course
Exercises and techniques to manage stress and anxiety.
Build success in your life by goal setting, relaxation and changing thinking with NLP
Free downloadable workbook
Kathryn Critchley
Skills Training Course
www.UoLearn.com

Coaching Skills Training Course
Your toolkit to coaching yourself and others with exercises and scripts
Downloadable templates ready to use
Kathryn Critchley

Order books from your favourite bookseller or direct from www.uolearn.com

Developing your assertiveness skills and confidence in your communication to achieve success.

How to build your confidence and assertiveness to handle difficult situations and people successfully. Increase your self esteem. Communicate your feelings and ideas and achieve your goals.

A Skills Training Course.
Lots of exercises and free downloadable workbook.

Published by: Universe of Learning Ltd, reg. number 6485477, Lancashire, UK
www.UoLearn.com, support@UoLearn.com

First Published 2013

ISBN 978-1-84937-057-8, UK spelling edition

Other editions:
ebook pdf format 978-1-84937-083-7
epub 978-1-84937-084-4
US spelling printed version: 978-1-84937-082-0

Photographs © www.fotolia.com
Edited by Dr Margaret Greenhall.

Praise

'This is the first time that I have really understood the difference between being aggressive and being assertive. This has helped me to develop new strategies for dealing with someone at work who I realise uses a lot of low level aggression to get what she wants.'

'Practical and engaging – I have already used several of the suggested ways to say no to great effect so thank you!'

'Learning to bank key phrases has helped me enormously. I always imagined that other people just knew how to deal with difficult situations, I now believe that with practice anyone can manage it.'

'The book has opened my eyes – I have recognised that a lot of things that I have blamed on other people can be traced back to my behaviour. I feel empowered and ready to take responsibility for my life.'

'I thought this book was excellent – readable and easy to work through. I particularly liked the chapter on self-confidence as I think that is where I need to do the work and so I have started an achievement log and am practising positive visualisation.'

Contents

About the Author: Deborah Dalley

Deborah has been working in the field of learning and development for over 25 years. Prior to setting up her own company in 2000 she worked as a training consultant for Greater Manchester Police and a part time lecturer at Salford University. The majority of Deborah's work involves helping people to find ways to deal with difficult situations. This includes running training workshops, coaching individuals and facilitating team events. She works in a range of organisations including many universities, local authorities, NHS trusts and private companies.

Her particular areas of interest and expertise include:

➤ Developing ways to improve organisational and personal communication. She has recently developed a framework for having difficult conversations which is being widely used in a number of organisations.

➤ Helping people to develop their ability to influence with integrity and to recognise the difference between effective influencing and manipulation.

➤ Ways to help leaders and managers cope with the challenges brought about by constant change.

Deborah is the co-author of Developing Your Influencing Skills, a book being used by organisations and individuals across the world.

Please contact Deborah at www.deborahdalley.com

Introduction

Have you ever walked away from a situation and thought why on earth didn't I speak up?

Have you ever agreed to do something because you did not know how to say no?

Have you ever lost your temper and regretted it afterwards?

Have you ever avoided a conversation because you were worried it might become confrontational?

Have you ever used sarcasm or silence to get your own way and then felt guilty?

If you answered yes to any of the above questions then this book will help you. Over the last twenty five years I have trained and coached thousands of people and something that most of us want to improve is our ability to say the right thing, to the right person, in the right way and at the right time.

The overall aims of the book are to:

- ✓ Provide an overview of the concept of assertiveness
- ✓ Help you to develop your self-confidence
- ✓ Give you a wide range of tools and techniques to use in everyday situations
- ✓ Help you to develop strategies for dealing with difficult situations
- ✓ Enable you to develop an action plan to continue to develop your interpersonal effectiveness

This book has been written with several audiences in mind – it could be used by:

- ✓ Individuals that are interested in developing their interpersonal effectiveness
- ✓ Learning professionals who want to use the theory and exercises with groups in their training sessions
- ✓ Managers and coaches who will be able to use many of the exercises to help individuals think through ways to deal with a difficult situation

The book is a mixture of case studies, practical tips and exercises. There is space in the book to complete the exercises as you go along. If you prefer you can download a printable copy of all the exercises from www.uolearn.com.

Chapter 1:
What is Assertive Behaviour?

"Behaviour is a mirror in which
everyone displays their own image."
Johann Wolfgang Van Goethe

Chapter 1:
What is Assertive Behaviour?

This chapter will help you to:

✓ Define the four main behaviour types

✓ Explore which behaviours you exhibit most often

✓ Review the effect each type of behaviour has on us and other people

Behaviour definitions

We need to begin by exploring what different behaviours look like. This can help you to recognise which behaviours you are currently adopting and to identify which forms of behaviour you find difficult to deal with in others.

Most behaviour can be grouped into one of four broad types:

➢ High level aggression

➢ Low level aggression

➢ Submissive

➢ Assertive

At the start of assertive communication workshops I ask people to spend a few minutes discussing what these four groups of behaviour look and sound like. It is interesting how frequently people struggle with the boundary between forms of aggressive behaviour and assertive behaviour. The following descriptions are the ones that I am going to be using throughout this book.

High level aggression

This form of behaviour involves expressing your needs, wants or beliefs in a way that dismisses the rights and opinions of others. The aim of high level aggression is to get your own way, even if that is at the expense of someone else. When we adopt this behaviour we ignore the views and feelings of others either intentionally or by default.

Some of the characteristics and behaviours that are associated with high level aggression include:

➢ Shouting or a loud voice

➢ Pointing fingers

➢ Foot tapping

➢ Threatening and intimidating behaviour

➢ Extreme impatience

➢ Invading someone's personal space

➢ Excessive eye contact

➢ Not listening to views that contradict our own

➢ Stating opinions as facts

➢ Advice in the form of 'should' or 'ought'

➢ Interrupting

Low level aggression

This is also behaviour that violates the rights of others in order to get what you want. Low level aggression is used to express annoyance or hostility without directly confronting the issue. It often involves trying to control others in a manipulative way by using sarcasm, silence or excessive flattery. As with high level aggression it is based on the belief that it is alright to get your own way with little regard for how that makes the other person feel.

Some of the characteristics and behaviours that are associated with low level aggression include:

➢ Making indirect responses

➢ Sarcastic comments

➢ Barbed humour

➢ Manipulative flattery

➢ Being two faced

➢ Refusing to make eye contact – looking away rather than down

➢ Cajoling

➢ Putting someone on the spot

➢ Refusing to speak to someone – using silence as a weapon

➢ Patronising behaviour

➢ Using language that infers guilt

➢ Gossiping about people

Submissive

Behaving submissively means ignoring your own needs and feelings and giving into others. It involves failing to stand up for your own rights or doing so in such a way that other people disregard them. This is usually done to avoid confrontation or to please others and often results in us ending up situations that we are not happy with. Often when we behave submissively we hope that the other person will know or guess what we really want and are then disappointed when they don't! Submissive behaviour is based on the belief that other people's needs, wants and opinions are more important than your own.

Some of the characteristics and behaviours that are associated with submission include:

➢ Minimal eye contact – often looking down

➢ Over justification

➢ Hesitant, quiet voice often dropping away at the end

➢ Excessive use of the word sorry

➢ Giving in easily

➢ Blaming others or self blame

➢ Difficulty making decisions or taking responsibility

➢ Not expressing own views or feelings

Assertive

Assertive behaviour means being honest with yourself and others. It means being able to say what you want but not at the expense of the other person. It is about being able to negotiate and reach workable compromises. Assertion is based on the belief that the needs, wants and opinions of both people matter.

Some of the characteristics and behaviours that are associated with assertion include:

✓ Steady, medium pitched voice

✓ Being prepared to compromise and look for common ground

✓ Regular eye contact but without staring

✓ Relaxed posture

✓ Treating people with respect

✓ Using open questions

✓ Smiling when appropriate

✓ Active listening

✓ Taking responsibility for ourselves and our actions

✓ Being trustworthy

✓ Behaving consistently

✓ Matching words, tone and body language

Exercise – How do you behave?

This exercise will help you to identify your behaviour patterns - look at the following questions and tick any that you think describe your behaviour.

Thinking about your current behaviour, tick a statement if you agree with it more than you disagree with it.

	Behaviour	✓
1	Do you tend to keep people waiting for you?	❑
2	Can you express your feelings openly and honestly?	❑
3	Do you apologise for things that are not your responsibility?	❑
4	Do you find it hard to highlight poor service?	❑
5	Do you often get into arguments?	❑
6	Do you regularly use sarcasm to make a point?	❑
7	Do you find it easy to admit that you have made a mistake?	❑
8	Do you get bad service corrected without making a fuss?	❑
9	Do you find it difficult to accept compliments?	❑
10	Do you gossip about people?	❑
11	Do you find it difficult to accept criticism?	❑
12	Do you let the other person finish before you begin speaking?	❑
13	Do you withhold information from people?	❑
14	Are you quick to blame yourself when things go wrong?	❑
15	Do you find it hard to 'back down'?	❑
16	Do you sometimes refuse to talk to someone for a while if they have upset you?	❑
17	Do you look for common ground in arguments?	❑
18	Do you tend to talk more than you listen?	❑
19	Do you feel that you have to make an excuse if you turn down an invitation?	❑

	Behaviour	✓
20	Do you often find that you pretend to listen when you are waiting to speak?	❑
21	Do you often find yourself going along with something when you don't want to?	❑
22	Can you usually resolve personal differences without damaging the relationship?	❑
23	Do you sometimes appear to co-operate but then undermine progress behind the scenes?	❑
24	Do you avoid conflict?	❑
25	Do you find it difficult to 'suffer fools gladly'?	❑
26	Do you agree with things in meetings or during conversations and then complain about them afterwards?	❑
27	Do you find it easy to tell people what you want without sounding harsh or abrupt?	❑
28	Do you try to listen and understand other people's points of view even if they are quite different to yours?	❑
29	Do you ever praise or flatter someone to get them to do what you want?	❑
30	Are you quick to blame others when something goes wrong?	❑
31	Do you find it difficult to express your feelings?	❑
32	Do you often step in and make decisions for other people?	❑
33	Do you usually have confidence in your own judgement?	❑
34	Do you often avoid people or situations for fear of embarrassment?	❑
35	Do you usually think you have the right answer?	❑
36	Do you sometimes send messages by email or text that you know you would not say to someone's face?	❑

The questions are linked to each behaviour type - circle the question numbers that you ticked.

High level aggression	5	11	15	18	20	25	30	32	35
Low level aggression	1	6	10	13	16	23	26	29	36
Submissive	3	4	9	14	19	21	24	31	34
Assertive	2	7	8	12	17	22	27	28	33

Are you predominately behaving in one manner or have the questions shown a range of behaviours?

What are your thoughts about this?

Recognising the four behaviours

As well as thinking about your own behaviour, it is also important to observe the way other people behave. The next exercise will help you to identify the four forms of behaviour. Solutions are given at the end of the exercise.

Exercise – Recognising behaviours

In each of the following scenarios there is a description of a situation and then four possible responses. Look at each response and state whether it is high level aggression, low level aggression, submissive or assertive.

Example:

You want to take this Friday off work because you have been offered tickets to an event you would really like to go to. You need to ask your manager if you can have the day off as leave.

	Response	Behaviour
A	Would it be possible for me to take leave on Friday? I appreciate it is short notice, however, I've been offered tickets for a concert which I would really like to go to.	**Assertive** *[This is a clear direct request explanation because it is short notice.]*
B	I won't be in on Friday. I'm taking leave.	**High level aggression** *[This is abrupt and takes no account of the other person's point of view.]*
C	Hi, I'm really sorry to bother you, I know you are busy. I was wondering whether there was any chance I could have Friday off - do say if it's a problem.	**Submissive** *[This is very apologetic and the language is non-assertive.]*
D	Can I ask a really big favour? I'm in a real dilemma. I need Friday off work. I know we are supposed to give a week's notice but Clare didn't last month so I was hoping you could possibly bend the rules again.	**Low Level aggression** *[The language is very exaggerated and the final comment is manipulative.]*

Situation 1:

You and your partner have just bought a new tent – it cost a lot of money and you have only used it once. A friend asks if she and her boyfriend can borrow it next weekend to go to a festival – you really do not want to lend it to them.

	Response	Behaviour
A	Well the thing is it cost a lot of money and we have only used it once and I am not sure if we need it that weekend.	
B	You are joking I wouldn't trust you with a £500 tent at a festival!	
C	I am sorry, no – we have decided that we are not going to lend it to anyone.	
D	I think it is a bit unfair of you to ask, you know we have only just bought it how would you feel if someone asked you to borrow something like that?	

Situation 2:

Your partner has forgotten your birthday.

	Response	Behaviour
A	Remind him or her and suggest going out for a meal to celebrate.	
B	Sulk until he or she asks you what is wrong and then say 'Nothing'.	
C	Carry on as though everything is fine but feel hurt.	
D	Shout at them	

19

Situation 3:

You are in the cinema and the group that are sitting behind you keep talking and laughing and they are spoiling your enjoyment of the film.

		Response	Behaviour
	A	Turn round and tell them to shut up.	
	B	Ask them to keep the noise down because you are trying to listen.	
	C	Keep turning round and glaring at them.	
	D	Say nothing and feel really annoyed.	

Situation 4

You are in a meeting at work and your manager suggests a new way of doing something that you are not convinced will work.

		Response	Behaviour
	A	Keep quiet in the meeting and afterwards moan to your colleagues.	
	B	Say in the meeting 'Well obviously that won't work; it's a stupid idea.'	
	C	Not say anything in the meeting or after.	
	D	During the meeting outline your concerns and ask others what their views are.	

Situation 5

You have been served lukewarm food in a restaurant.

	Response	Behaviour
A	Call the waiter over and explain that the food is not as hot as you would expect it to be and ask him or her to bring you another one.	
B	Call the waiter over and say 'If I had wanted cold food I would have ordered a salad – this is completely unacceptable - get it sorted'.	
C	Say nothing, eat the food and feel disappointed that it was not as good as you had hoped.	
D	Complain to the people at your table in a loud voice and hope the waiter/waitress overhears.	

Situation	A	B	C	D
1	Submissive	High level aggression	Assertive	Low level aggression
2	Assertive	Low level aggression	Submissive	High level aggression
3	High level aggression	Assertive	Low level aggression	Submissive
4	Low level aggression	High level aggression	Submissive	Assertive
5	Assertive	High level aggression	Submissive	Low level aggression

How easy did you find it to recognise the different forms of behaviour?

....

....

Behaviour breeds behaviour

So does it really matter? We all know people who have carved very successful careers on aggressive forms of behaviour. It is for you to choose how you want to live your life but it is important to recognise that the behaviour that you exhibit will have an effect on how people behave towards you.

The effects of submissive behaviour

'If people are using you like a doormat then this is because you have let them do so' Lynda Field

In the short term submissive behaviour can feel quite positive, at the time you avoid confrontation and it often keeps other people happy. However, the more we suppress our own needs, the more resentful and undervalued we begin to feel. This continued avoidance becomes a self defeating cycle that can result in a loss of self-confidence and the development of a victim mentality. Over the longer term, this can lead to increased stress levels and sudden aggressive outbursts.

In many instances other people find submissive behaviour quite frustrating because they do not know what you want. This can lead to your ideas and feelings being ignored and others not taking you seriously.

The effects of high level aggressive behaviour

'Force is all conquering but its victories are short lived'

The immediate effect of using this type of behaviour is that you may get what you want and this can induce a feeling of power and victory. However, this success is often short lived as people quickly start to resent you and this can lead to feelings of increased isolation which in turn can lead to stress.

If high level aggression is used for any length of time others become very wary of you and will start to avoid you. It also leads to strong levels of resentment and a lack of respect. If you have ever lived or worked with someone that adopts this behaviour you will have noticed how much it can affect the way people around them behave. The atmosphere becomes very tense as people are afraid of making a mistake or saying the wrong thing.

The effects of low level aggressive behaviour

'The moment there is suspicion about a person's motives everything they do becomes tainted' Mahatma Ghandi

Low level aggression allows us to express our displeasure with something or someone without being directly confrontational. This can feel quite satisfying particularly when we get others to collude. Longer term though if we continue to deal with things behind people's backs, gossip or make snide comments it can begin to make us feel uncomfortable. This sort of behaviour often has the short-term effect of making others feel that they are the ones in the wrong because they do not really understand what is going on. If the behaviour continues, this changes. The people around become confused, irritated and resentful – this often turns to anger. Any form of sustained manipulation leads to a breakdown of trust in relationships.

The effects of assertive behaviour

'We teach people the way we want them to treat us.'

Behaving assertively increases self-confidence. You start to achieve things through open and honest dialogue and don't spend a disproportionate amount of time dwelling on things that are out of your control. This ultimately leads to higher levels of self-esteem and consequently less stress. People will trust and respect you - this is because they believe that you mean what you say.

Assertiveness is not the answer to all your communication problems. It is a set of behaviours, tools and techniques that can help you to deal more effectively with situations that you find difficult and thereby reduce the anger, frustration and anxiety they can cause. By learning to be more assertive in our relationships we begin to take more control of our lives.

In summary assertive behaviour:

✓ Relies on honesty and integrity

✓ Is about clear, direct and open communication

✓ Protects your rights and respects the rights of other people

✓ Helps to develop your self esteem

✓ Looks for jointly agreed solutions that both parties are happy with

✓ Enables you to tell people what you would like to happen

✓ Balances your needs with those of others

Why do we find it difficult to be assertive?

It is important to remember that many things about our past and upbringing can influence our adult behaviour. If as a child being 'good' meant being seen and not heard then it can be difficult to override those messages - if you were rewarded for 'not making a fuss' or 'fitting in' then those submissive forms of behaviour become the ones that we repeat in our adult lives. Similarly, if as a child you found the best way to get attention was to scream and shout then it can be hard to change that behaviour. Many children work out at an early age that sulking or flattery are the best way to get what they want and so those low level aggressive behaviours may continue into adulthood.

We all form habits and patterns in our behaviour and relationships and sometimes these can be difficult for us to break. If you have always reacted in a particular way to something then it will take some work to change that – firstly we have to recognise the habit, then decide if we are happy with it and if not decide how to change it.

'I am your constant companion. I am your greatest helper or heaviest burden. I will push you onward or drag you down to failure. I am completely at your command. Half the things you do you might just as well turn over to me, and I will be able to do them quickly, correctly. I am easily managed – you must merely be firm with me. Show me exactly how you want something done, and after a few lessons I will do it automatically. I am the servant of all great people; and alas of failures as well. Those who are failures, I have made failures. I am not a machine although I work with all the precision of a machine plus the intelligence of a human being. You may run me for a profit or turn me for ruin - it makes no difference to me. Take me, train me, be firm with me and I will place the world at your feet. Be easy with me and I will destroy you.

Who am I? I am a habit.'

Author unknown

Exercise – Behaviour action plan

After reading this chapter you will hopefully have a better understanding of the four forms of behaviour.

Spend a few minutes thinking about any of the aggressive or submissive behaviours that you would like to stop using.

I would like to stop........

....
....
....
....
....
....
....

Now spend a few minutes identifying any of the assertive behaviours that you would like to start using more.

I would like to start...

....
....
....
....
....
....
....

Chapter Two:
Self-Confidence

'Whether you think that you can or that you can't,
you are usually right.' Henry Ford

Chapter Two:
Self-Confidence

This chapter will help you to:

✓ Examine the role of 'rights' in being assertive

✓ Identify the things that stop you behaving assertively

✓ Find ways to challenge some of your fears

✓ Explore ways to build your self-belief and confidence

Our rights

Assertiveness is based on a fundamental belief that as human beings we have certain personal rights. These are the underlying values that we expect people to respect when dealing with us. It is important to recognise that this is a two way process. If we want people to acknowledge and respect our personal rights, we have to treat others in the same way. When you are behaving assertively you stand up for your rights and express them in a clear and appropriate way. You also recognise your responsibility to protect the rights of other people. Look at the following list and consider whether you believe you have these rights.

I believe I have the right to:

- ❑ My own opinions, views and ideas
- ❑ A fair hearing for those ideas
- ❑ Have needs or wants that may be different to other peoples
- ❑ Ask (not demand) that others respond to my needs and wants
- ❑ Refuse a request without feeling guilty or selfish
- ❑ Express my feelings appropriately
- ❑ Decide not to assert myself (i.e. choose not to raise a particular issue)
- ❑ Be myself
- ❑ Be successful
- ❑ Have my rights respected

During training sessions most people will look at this list and say 'Well, yes, I agree in principle but it is not always that easy – I can't tell my boss that I am not going to do my work because it is my right not to want to do it!' and of course that is true. However, it is critical to begin to recognise when and with whom you allow your rights to be taken away because these are the situations in which you will struggle to behave assertively. Of course your manager has the right to ask you to do something and equally you do have the right to voice your opinion as long as you do it in an appropriate way.

Do you also take responsibility for respecting the rights of others?

I believe other people have the right to:

- ❑ Their own opinions and ideas, even if they are not the same as mine
- ❑ Be listened to
- ❑ Refuse a request from me
- ❑ Express their feelings appropriately
- ❑ Be themselves
- ❑ Be successful
- ❑ Have different needs and wants to mine

Case study

During the session on rights at an assertiveness workshop Karen asked if she could share her story with the group. Her son was being bullied at school – on a number of occasions he had been called names, had bits of his lunch taken from him and had been ignored in the playground by his classmates. Karen found the headmaster of the school quite intimidating and was slightly in awe of him. Despite this, she was very clear that the way her son was being treated was unacceptable and so she arranged a meeting with the Head to discuss her son's treatment. The meeting had gone very well and Karen was happy that she had been quite firm and clear about how she wanted things to change. It was only afterwards that she realised that her manager had been bullying her for years – he regularly shouted at her, often asked her to work through her lunch hour and did not always share vital information with her in order for her to do her job properly. In fact, these were very similar problems to those that her son had been experiencing.

Does this sound familiar?

What Karen's story illustrates is that we often find it much easier to assert rights for someone else. So although Karen had behaved assertively when she believed her son was being treated unfairly she knew that she would be very unlikely to have the same conversation with her manager about the way he treated her.

So to become more assertive in a given situation we need to:

- ✓ Believe that we have the right.
- ✓ Have the confidence, in that situation, to assert that right.
- ✓ Be able to assert that right in a reasonable and responsible way.
- ✓ Respect the rights of others.

There will be many situations in which you already behave assertively. These are the occasions when you are clear about what you want and feel confident and able to express that. It is the other times that you need to work on, before reading any further stop and consider the people and situations that you find difficult to deal with.

Exercise - Where do you need to do the work?

The list below is divided into people and situations – as you look down the list tick the ones that you would like to work on.

People with whom I would like to behave more assertively:

☐ Manager
☐ Figures of authority
☐ Parents
☐ Children
☐ Partner
☐ Friends
☐ Colleagues
☐ Members of staff
☐ Siblings
☐ Other relatives
☐ Strangers
☐ Neighbours
☐ High pressure sales people

List any others here:

....

....

Situations in which I would like to behave more assertively:

☐ Meetings
☐ Restaurants / shops
☐ Unfamiliar places
☐ Large social groups
☐ Family gatherings
☐ Interviews
☐ Presentations

List any others here:

....

....

Facing your fears

Before you can begin to behave assertively you need to start to think assertively. In the last exercise you identified some of the situations in which you find it difficult to do or say what you think because you are not sure that you have the right. This is only part of the story, I have worked with many people who genuinely believe they have the right but do not have the confidence to assert that right.

Exercise – What stops you?

Think about all the times in your life when you have not made a change, tackled a situation or avoided a conversation because you did not have the confidence to do it.

What stopped you?

....
....
....
....
....
....
....

What were you afraid might happen as a result?

....
....
....
....
....
....
....

When groups do this exercise in workshops the list usually looks something like this:

- ✗ I worried that I might make the situation worse
- ✗ I did not want to fall out with her
- ✗ I was afraid I might lose my job
- ✗ I was worried that it wouldn't work and I would be worse off
- ✗ I didn't want to have an argument
- ✗ I didn't want to look stupid
- ✗ I was afraid that I might be wrong and make a fool of myself
- ✗ I was concerned that they might not like the idea
- ✗ I would have felt embarrassed if other people didn't agree with me
- ✗ I was worried that I might offend them
- ✗ I didn't want to upset anyone
- ✗ I didn't want to make a fuss

As Susan Jeffers explains in her bestselling book 'Feel the Fear and Do it Anyway' the root of most of our fears is that we think we won't be able to handle a situation. This results in these fears paralysing us because we believe that we will not be able to deal with the outcome. Therefore, it is the mastery of our fears that really matters. If we reach a point where we believe we can handle the outcome we no longer fear it. The way to begin to manage and control our fears is to develop our self-confidence.

'The only thing we have to fear is fear itself' Franklin Roosevelt

What is self-confidence?

Our self-confidence is based on a judgement we make about our ability to achieve things. We feel confident when we believe that we can do something and do it well.

Our thoughts, feeling and behaviour are interrelated and so if our thoughts about something are negative, this inevitably affects the way we feel, which in turn affects our behaviour.

Picture this:

Diane is due to give an important presentation to a group of prospective clients. She lay awake for ages last night thinking about it and did not fall asleep until the early hours – as a result of this she overslept. This meant that she didn't have time to do her final run through this morning or check that the PowerPoint slides were all in the right order. She runs down the corridor to get to the board room on time. As she enters the room she is picturing all the things that could go wrong – this makes her very nervous and she starts to feel a bit sick and her hands begin to shake. She stands up and says 'Good morning everyone' – her voice is tremulous and a bit squeaky.

Mike is in the board room when Diane arrives – she is a few minutes late which is really unlike her. He also notices that she looks very pale and a bit worried, as she walks into the room she doesn't smile at anyone. Mike is concerned and is thinking 'I hope Diane is OK, I wonder if something has gone wrong at home I must catch her afterwards and ask if everything is alright.'

Diane looks at the audience; Mike is looking really serious and a bit confused. She starts to panic – 'Why is Mike looking so worried this must be going really badly, I knew that I wasn't ready.........................'

Do you recognise this cycle? This is a typical example of how our self-confidence becomes eroded if we do not believe we have the ability to do something well – it very quickly becomes a self-fulfilling prophecy.

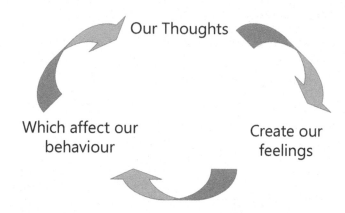

So when our thoughts are negative, we feel pessimistic and this often results in behaviour that leads to a poor outcome which reinforces the thought that started the process.

It therefore follows that if we do believe we can do something that leads to optimistic expectations which result in positive behaviour that is more likely to lead to success.

The interdependency of our thoughts, feelings and behaviour means that if we consciously change any one of the three, we can transform the nature of the experience.

The good news is that anyone can increase their self-confidence. I have worked with hundreds of people who have wanted to change something or do something differently but have become 'stuck'. The key to them moving forward is nearly always in helping them to develop the confidence to do it.

Remember, this means finding a way to believe that you have the ability to achieve success.

Ways to develop your self-confidence

Different approaches work with different people and so here are 12 of the confidence building techniques that I use to help people. Some will work for you and others may not, don't worry about that, find the ones that you think will help you.

1. Create a support network

Spend time with people who help and encourage your self-belief rather than those that undermine it. Negativity attracts more negativity. Make a conscious decision to spend more time with the people that make you feel good.

Exercise – Your support network

List all the people in your support network who foster your self-belief. Do not include the people that undermine you.

....

....

....

....

....

....

If your list is quite small think about how you could expand it e.g. join a club, an on-line forum or a business network

*'Keep away from people who try to belittle your ambitions.
Small people always do that, but the really great
make you feel that you too can become great' Mark Twain*

2. Challenge your fears

When you identify fears that are stopping you ask yourself are they rational or irrational? When you identify an irrational belief, challenge it and ask yourself two questions:

Where is the evidence for what I am thinking?

What is the logic in my interpretation?

This is critical because if we do not question our own negative self-talk it saps our self-belief and we fall into faulty thinking that sounds like this 'Well it is not worth taking the risk because it will probably go wrong and if I have tried and failed I will feel worse than I do now.'

When you identify a fear that is rational you need to decide whether there is anything that you can do to diminish it. For many people this is about acknowledging the fears and then identifying the steps to make them manageable.

It is really important not to get lost in vague, foggy fears because when we do we can very quickly let our thoughts spiral out of control.

When dealing something you are anxious about ask yourself the question,

"What is the worst that could happen and how would I deal with that?"

Once you've identified the fears you can begin to develop strategies to overcome them.

*'One important key to success is self-confidence.
An important key to self-confidence is preparation.' Arthur Ashe*

Case study

Farah had been at home for the last five years looking after her two small children. She had decided that she would like to return to some paid work – having spent six months applying for part time jobs she had finally got an interview. She admitted that she was really scared about it and had almost convinced herself that it wasn't worth going for the interview because she wouldn't get the job anyway. I asked her to list all the things that she was worried about – the list is reproduced below:

➢ I am worried that I will not be able to find the place as it is in the centre of town.
➢ I have no idea what to wear.
➢ My skills and experience are 5 years out of date.
➢ I won't be able to answer the questions.
➢ I won't be able to think of anything intelligent to ask them.
➢ If I don't get it I will have to tell everyone that I failed.
➢ If I do get it who will look after the children?

Once Farah had identified the fears she started to put together a plan to make them manageable. This included:

✓ Doing a dry run of the journey the Sunday before the interview – drive into town and find the building and identify a car park.
✓ Talk to friends about outfits and see if someone will lend me something to wear.
✓ Download a list of typical interview questions from the internet and practise answering them.
✓ Prepare several questions to ask at the interview.
✓ Research local nursery provision / talk to my mother in law about helping.
✓ Visualise the interview going really well

What Farah had begun to do was focus her attention on things she had some control over and as soon as she started to do that her confidence grew.

3. Visualise success

When we are thinking about doing something we perceive as difficult we tend to focus on all the things that could go wrong. This results in all our energy following that negative focus. Imagine how much more powerful it would be to channel all that energy into making it go well. Ask yourself what would it look like if I handled this situation really well? How would I be behaving? What would the outcome be? What do I need to do to ensure that happens?

Many people struggle with the concept of visualisation and will argue that they cannot do it. If you are one of those people try the following exercise.

Exercise - Visualisation

Imagine that you are walking down the road and you pass a beautiful cottage with flowers round the door.
What colour are the flowers?

....

The front door opens and a child walks out.
How old is the child?

....

The child bends down and picks up a toy.
What does the toy look like?

....

You have probably got quite a strong image in your mind now – that is visualisation. Practise this with all kinds of situations.

Exercise - Visualisation

Think about a situation that you find difficult to handle at the moment. Spend some time imagining yourself being very successful and happy with how you deal with it.

....

....

....

....

4. Congratulate yourself

Human beings have evolved to spend more time thinking about negative experiences than positive ones. Our brain tends to focus by default on what has gone wrong and how we could put it right. The following exercise can help to direct your thoughts away from the negative towards the positive.

Exercise - Reflect on your success

Every night for the next week, before you go to sleep, reflect on two things:

1. Ask yourself 'What have I done well today?'. Identify anything that you are pleased with - remember the events you choose can be small things – for example:
'I was pleased with the way the presentation went this afternoon'
'I thought the meal I cooked tonight was really nice.'

2. Remember any praise you have received during the day, repeat it to yourself and congratulate yourself.

5. Keep a record of your achievements

Many people will only start to list their achievements if they are updating their CV in order to apply for a job. One way to strengthen your self-confidence is to start to acknowledge things that you have achieved so keep a log of the following:

- ✓ Courses that you have attended
- ✓ Qualifications that you have gained
- ✓ New skills that you have developed – physical, mental and interpersonal skills
- ✓ Projects that you have been involved in (these can be at home or work)
- ✓ Community activities
- ✓ Voluntary work
- ✓ Email/letters of thanks

6. Avoid the blame game

Try to stop blaming yourself, or others, when things go wrong. If you regularly 'beat yourself up' for mistakes that you have made you will be doing a good job of undermining your own self-confidence. If you make a mistake learn from it – reflect on what happened and decide how you would do it differently next time and then move on!

7. Learn more

There are many excellent books and websites that explore ways to develop self-esteem and self-confidence – some of my favourites are listed below.

Feel the Fear and Do It Anyway by Susan Jeffers

Awaken the Giant Within by Tony Robbins

The Self Esteem Workbook by Lynda Field

Ten Steps to Positive Living by Windy Dryden

www.centreforconfidence.co.uk

8. Work within your circle of influence

It is important for your self-confidence that you work on things that you do have some power to influence – if you spend a lot of time worrying or complaining about things which you cannot do anything about you will be expending a lot of time and energy for nothing. This inevitably reduces our belief that we have any control over our own lives. If you have a problem that you can do something about, do it – if you cannot do anything about it, it's a fact, so incorporate it into your plans.

9. Project a positive image

Remember behaviour breeds behaviour.

If you walk down the road and you smile at someone what are they most likely to do? Smile back – how does that make you feel? Although this is very obvious, we often forget the power our behaviour has on other people. If you are sarcastic or offhand with someone the chances are their behaviour will mirror yours. If you begin to drive aggressively some drivers will start to compete with you. If you start to project a positive image it will not only encourage positive behaviour from others it will make you feel more confident.

Think about what your posture is projecting – do you stand up straight and make eye contact with people when you are speaking to them? Do you sound enthusiastic when you are talking?

Decide to start acting in a very confident way in one small area e.g. walking to the car, saying no to cold telephone callers, asking for help in a shop.

Start to dress the part – if you believe that you look the part you will feel more confident.

Ensure that you are using positive language:

'I am getting better at this'...........not 'I am useless at this.'

'How can I do this?'............................not 'Why can't I do this?'

'What has that taught me' ....not 'When will I ever learn?'

43

10. Break things down

Question: How do you eat an elephant?

Answer: One bite at a time

This old joke has become a maxim for the way we need to deal with problems and issues that seem too big to handle, if we try to tackle the whole thing we can become overwhelmed by the enormity of the task. This often results in us putting it off which then leads to a feeling of frustration and failure which always has a negative impact on self-confidence.

When facing something big we need to start with a bite, this involves breaking the overall goal into a list of manageable actions and identifying the first steps. These steps need to be small enough to be achieved easily and quickly, this leads to action and progress which makes us feel good and bolsters our self-confidence.

For example:

Goal: To lose weight

Actions:

➢ Find out what I weigh now and set a target weight
➢ Decide whether to join a slimming club
➢ Clear out the food cupboards to get rid of the chocolate, biscuits etc.
➢ Plan weekly food menus and make shopping lists
➢ Weigh myself weekly and keep a progress chart
➢ Devise an exercise plan
➢ Set an interim goal weight

First Steps:

✓ Weigh myself tonight and start a chart
✓ Take some photos to put on the fridge
✓ Look on the internet to see which slimming clubs are running meetings in my area

11. Affirmations

The word affirm means to make firm, so positive affirmations are statements that people make in order to change the way that they feel about something. Some people do this by writing the affirmation down over and over again, others by saying it and some do it by cutting out a picture of what they want, carrying it round and looking at it regularly.

Affirmations can have a profound effect on how you feel. They must be in the present tense and focus on what you do want not on what you don't want.

Some examples of affirmations:

I am happy and healthy

I have a fulfilling and satisfying job

I have a lot of energy

12. Be your own best friend

Talk to yourself in the same way that you would talk to your best friend. We tend to be far more critical of ourselves than we do of others. Be tolerant of your mistakes in the way you would be of others.

Exercise – Strengthening your self-confidence

Look back over the 12 ways to develop confidence and identify 3 things that you are going to do.

Action 1:
First step:

Action 2:
First step:

Action 3:
First step:

'As we let our light shine, we unconsciously give other people permission to do the same. As we are liberated from our own fear our presence automatically liberates others.' Nelson Mandela

Chapter Three:
Assertive
Communication Skills

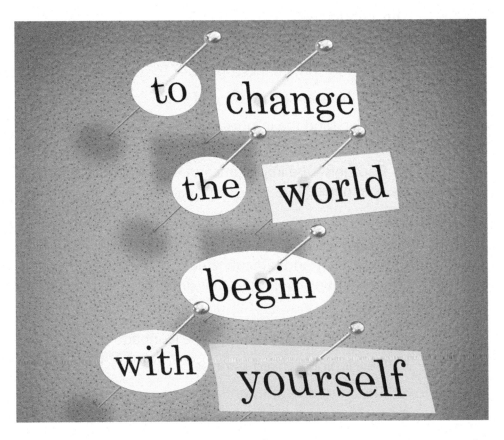

'Communication works for those who work at it.'
John Powell

Chapter Three: Assertive Communication Skills

This chapter will help you to:

- ✓ Choose the words to use when acting assertively
- ✓ Develop some banked phrases to use in difficult situations
- ✓ Use the appropriate tone of voice
- ✓ Understand the importance of body language in assertive behaviour
- ✓ Recognise the importance of listening skills to assertive communication

In the next chapter we will look at specific techniques for dealing with everyday and difficult situations. However, there are five core communication skills that underpin assertive behaviour.

They are:

1. The ability to use appropriate language
2. Developing banked phrases
3. Choosing the right tone of voice
4. Ensuring congruent body language
5. Listening actively

1. Using appropriate language

Assertive language is clear and direct without being aggressive, it focuses on what can be done rather than what can't. It is almost impossible to give people the 'right' words to use because one of the most important things about clear communication is that you use language and phrases that sound like you. This is all part of the honesty and integrity that is central to developing an assertive approach. There are, however, some pitfalls that you need to avoid when choosing the words that you are going to use.

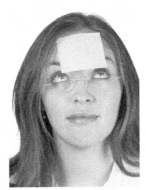

Pitfall 1: Excessive apologising

A habit that many of us have picked up over the years is the over use of the word 'sorry'. For some of us a sentence isn't complete if it doesn't have a sorry in it somewhere.

Have you ever walked into a parking meter and apologised?

Without doubt there are times when it is appropriate to apologise, if you have done something wrong, upset someone or made a mistake. However, if you are saying sorry all the time for things that are not your fault or responsibility the meaning of the word becomes diluted and then when we are genuinely sorry we have no way to express that. Often people will defend their use of the word sorry as being polite but it is important to recognise how much it can undermine your position.

If every time you approach your manager you start by saying 'Sorry to bother you............'. Just stop and ask yourself what am I apologising for? Have you done something wrong? Have you hurt their feelings?' 'Have you upset them?' The chances are you are simply asking them to do their job so why start by apologising?

For many people this is a habit that started in childhood and like all habits it can be broken.

Have a look at the following everyday examples:

➢ Approaching your manager
Instead of saying 'Sorry to bother you but...............'
Try using 'Excuse me, have you got a moment?'

➢ Asking a favour
Instead of 'I am really sorry to ask but I was wondering if you could...'
Try using 'I was hoping you might be able to do me a favour, could you..........'

> **Exercise – Saying sorry**
>
> Listen to yourself over the next few weeks and notice the times that you say sorry. Each time consider:
>
> What am I apologising for? If the answer is 'nothing' then consider what you could have said instead of sorry.

Pitfall 2: 'But ....'

The use of the word 'but' often has quite negative connotations – as soon as we hear someone saying 'Yes, but....' we assume that they are going to contradict what has just been said. In most instances 'but' can be easily replaced with however, and, also, or next – these all sound as though you are building on an idea rather than rejecting it. Look at the two phrases below and consider which sounds more positive

'That is a great idea but I think we need to focus on......'

'That is a great idea and I think we also need to focus on....'

The chances are the second option will keep the conversation open and moving forward whereas there is a danger with the first option that the other person becomes quite defensive and the conversation will then become more difficult.

Pitfall 3: Vague generalisations

In an attempt to avoid sounding too direct or abrupt we can end up being so vague that our language becomes at best open to misinterpretation and at worst meaningless.

➢ What do the following mean?

'Could you get it to me as soon as possible?'
You really do need to improve your timekeeping'
'You need to pull your socks up.'

2. Banked phrases

One thing that I have learned whilst working in this field is that most people find it difficult to think of the perfect phrase in the heat of the moment. How many times have you thought afterwards 'Why on earth didn't I say................?' This is not surprising because when we are feeling under pressure it is very hard to find the right words. It is therefore a good idea to start 'banking' phrases in your mind that you have practised over and over again to use when situations arise. As you work through the next chapter you will find lots of examples but here are a few that people have practised and 'banked' on previous training courses.

Examples:

Siobhan's mother regularly rings at 6.30pm in the evening just as Siobhan is trying to bath her children – she always wants to chat and Siobhan finds it really hard to get her off the phone

Siobhan's banked phrase – 'Hi Mum, good to hear from you, the kids are in the bath at the moment – I will ring you back as soon as the children are in bed so that we can have a proper chat'

The photocopier for the department is in Val's office although it is not part of her job to photocopy for other people. She has put some clear instructions on the machine explaining how to use it however people still come in and hand her things and ask to have them copied.

Val's banked phrase – 'It is a self service machine so please help yourself – I have put some instructions on the wall, if you have any problems give me a shout.'

3. Tone of voice

The words are only part of the story – you can convey a whole range of meanings by altering the pace, pitch, tone, volume or emphasis in your delivery.

Let's take a fairly simple sentence

'I have got a huge amount of work to get through so really can't chat now.'

➤ Say this sentence in a quiet, hesitant, apologetic way

➤ Now say it again in a loud, belligerent way emphasising the words huge and really.

➤ Now say it in a sarcastic way with emphasis on the 'I have'.

➤ Now say it in a level, mid-pitch tone.

It is remarkable how the meaning of sixteen words can change so dramatically. If we are feeling any strong emotion it is often our tone of voice that is affected. Our 'inner voice' will leak out so it is important to separate the emotion from the content of what we want to say. If your inner voice is saying things like 'You are not going to get away with that' or 'I think you are a waste of space' then your tone of voice is likely to be aggressive without you even realising it. Similarly if the messages going through your mind are 'It really isn't worth the hassle' or 'What if they don't like me after this' then your tone is likely to betray that. If, on the other hand, what you are thinking is 'It's OK to say this' you will deliver the message in a clear and open and friendly manner.

Practising to breathe properly can help you to control the pace, pitch and volume of your voice. Often if we are nervous or concerned about something our breathing becomes shallower, we start to breathe high in the ribcage and the abdomen does not move at all. This can result in a shortage of breath which means that the words come out in a tumble and you run out of breath at the end of a sentence. Learning to breathe well can help you to calm yourself before starting a conversation that you are anxious about. Try the following exercise and see if you notice the difference.

Exercise - Calming yourself

Sit in an upright and comfortable position.

Close your eyes or lower them to the ground if you are somewhere too public

Breathe through your nose for a count of four.

Hold the breath for a count of seven.

Then exhale through your mouth for a count of eight – concentrate on pushing all the air out with your tummy muscles.

Repeat this five times

Practise this regularly and you will find that it becomes more automatic and will help to calm you and ensure that your voice remains even and measured.

4. Body language

The word congruence comes from a Latin word that means to come together, to agree. When we are behaving congruently our words, tone and body language are all saying the same thing and therefore we are giving a clear and consistent message. When we do this 99% of the meaning will come from the words because they are being supported by the other two. We often undermine ourselves by verbally saying one thing and non-verbally communicating something else. This gives a mixed message and when this happens the non-verbal element becomes the overriding one. The following diagram illustrates the impact each area has if they are not saying the same thing.

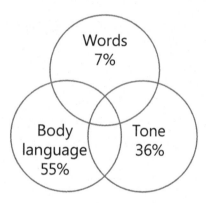

So when we give a mixed message the body language becomes the most dominant part of the communication.

Can you picture times when people have said things to you and you have felt or thought that they mean something else? Incongruence is noticeable and when we experience it we feel quite uncomfortable – do we believe the words or the non verbal message?

Examples of incongruence

➢ A manager that says 'My door is always open' but the reality is that they are constantly in meetings and it is difficult for staff to get time with them.

➢ A member of staff that sits in a meeting with their arms folded, staring out of the window looking bored and yet when asked if everything is alright says 'Yes, fine.'

➢ The friend that says 'You must tell me all about it, I really want to know' however as soon as you start talking they look uncomfortable and keep checking their watch.

If you want to develop a strong communication capability it is imperative that you ensure your delivery is congruent. We feel comfortable with people that behave in this way – we believe their message and we trust them.

The following non-verbal behaviours are usually associated with assertive behaviour:

➢ Confident eye contact is direct without becoming an aggressive stare. To appear positive and interested in what someone is saying your gaze needs to meet theirs about 60 – 70% of the time. Withdrawing eye contact is often interpreted as a signal of submission or a lack of interest.

➢ Non-verbal prompts demonstrate that we are listening and will help to make the other person feel comfortable – these can include affirmative head nodding and appropriate facial expressions including smiling if appropriate.

➢ Relaxing your own body will usually help the other person to relax too. If you are directly facing someone it can feel quite confrontational, turning your body slightly to the side can cause the other person to feel less defensive. Be aware of how close you are to someone when communicating – we all have an imaginary space round us which if entered uninvited can make us feel uncomfortable.

5. Listening

The final core skill in assertive behaviour is the willingness and ability to listen and compromise. This is an underpinning value of assertive behaviour because it is the point at which we acknowledge and respect the right of someone to have a different view to our own. True assertion is not about 'getting your own way', it is about finding a solution that both parties are comfortable with. We can start to do this by providing space for discussion, questions and feedback.

So what do we mean when we talk about really listening?

Below is the Chinese symbol for listening – I think the elements that make up the character really summarise what true listening is about.

The left section denotes the 'ear'

There are 4 sections on the right, the top one says 'you', the next is 'eyes', then 'undivided attention' and the last one is the 'heart'

Ears   聽   You   Eyes   Undivided attention   Heart

Barriers to listening

Although we take it for granted that we can listen there are many things that get in the way, the common barriers to active listening include the following:

➢ Most of us can think about four times faster than the average person can speak – this is to enable us to process the meaning of what they are saying. Sometimes we use this extra space to think about our own personal affairs or concerns rather than listening.

➢ There are certain words that can cause us to stop listening either because they irritate us or the subject bores us – these terms vary with individuals but can include things like 'should', 'politics', 'must', 'unions' etc. As soon as we hear them an automatic response is triggered and we phase out.

➢ Sometimes we decide in the first few seconds that we know what someone is going to say and so assume that we do not need to listen.

➢ If we don't agree with what someone else is saying we often stop listening because we start to prepare our counter argument rather than trying to understand their point of view.

➢ If ideas are too complex there is a danger that we shut off all together.

➢ When someone is saying something with a lot of facts in it we try to remember them by repeating them over and over in our head thereby creating a barrier to listening to the rest of the information.

➢ External distractions can prevent good listening – if there are other conversations going on round you or a lot of noise it can be hard to concentrate on the right thing.

Levels of listening

When we do listen there are a number of different levels that we can choose to engage at:

Level 1 – Waiting to speak

At this level we are not really interested in what the other person is saying we are only listening in order to interject, often to discuss something completely different. If you are in the office listening to two people discussing something that has nothing to do with you but you have a message for one of them you might be listening at level 1.

Level 2 – Listening to tell our story

This is the level that people often listen at in social situations. It is when the conversation is a series of stories and experiences that are loosely connected, when one person finishes their story the next person relates theirs and so it continues.

Level 3 – Listening to give advice

This is a slightly deeper level as at this point the listener is starting to try and understand what the other person is saying because they are going to advise them, or tell them, what action to take next.

Level 4 – Listening and asking for more

This is the point at which we move away from our own thoughts or views and really try to explore the other person's perspective. This involves asking questions to help clarify that we have gathered all the information about their viewpoint and involves us working to understand their thoughts and feelings about the issue.

Level 5 – Listening to understand

This is the deepest level of listening and involves picking up both the verbal and non verbal signals in order to fully understand someone's underlying beliefs and values about something.

Which level?

Deciding the appropriate level a situation requires is part of our day to day communication ability. If you are standing at the bus stop and someone comments on the weather it might be appropriate to listen at level 2, in fact if you started to listen at 4 or 5 the other person may wish they had not started the conversation!

The important thing to recognise is that when the outcome is important to us we need to shift to a deeper level of listening. This is because when we are listening at levels 1, 2 and 3 we are only seeing the world from our own perspective and this can make it very difficult to find common ground and areas for compromise. The more we focus on what we see differently the wider the gulf becomes. The minute we start to look for what we agree on dialogue begins.

This is not purely about understanding someone else's point of view it is also about assessing your willingness and ability to change your mind or compromise if necessary.

Exercise - Change and feedback

Spend a few minutes answering the following questions as honestly as possible:

When did you last change your mind after listening to someone else's point of view?

....

....

How comfortable are you with other people challenging your views?

....

....

How often do you ask others for feedback and then act on what they have told you?

....

....

---

*'He who knows only his own side of the case,
knows little of that' John Stuart Mill*

Chapter Four:
Assertiveness Techniques

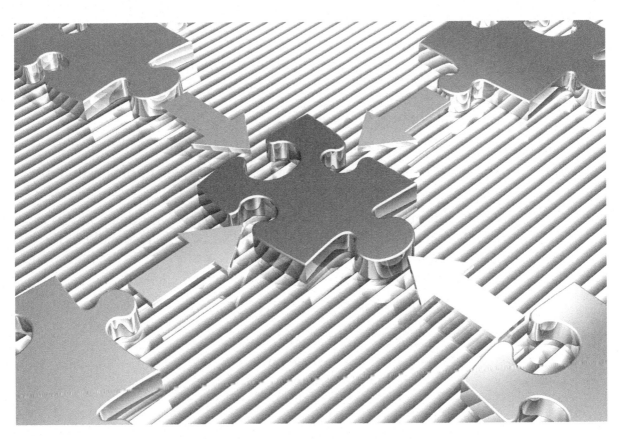

'Technique is the test of sincerity. If a thing isn't worth
getting the technique to say, it is of inferior value.'
Ezra Pound

Chapter Four: Assertiveness Techniques

This chapter will look at a range of assertiveness techniques for handling everyday and difficult situations.

This chapter will help you to:

✓ Identify the situations that you find difficult to deal with

✓ Develop a range of tools and techniques to deal with those situations assertively

At the start of communication workshops I ask delegates to list the situations that they would like to be able to handle more assertively. The most commonly cited ones are listed below and will be discussed in this chapter.

1. Making requests
2. Saying no
3. Raising awkward issues
4. Disagreeing with someone
5. Handling angry people
6. Being put on the spot
7. Standing your ground
8. Handling put downs
9. Responding to criticism
10. Dealing with negativity
11. Receiving compliments
12. Giving feedback

1. Making requests

This is an area where we are often our own worst enemy – rather than focusing clearly on the request that we want to make we start imagining the other person's reaction. Remember – you have the right to ask as long as you respect the other person's right to refuse.

When making requests:

- ✓ Be clear and specific – don't use words and phrases that are open to interpretation

- ✓ Be polite but do not over apologise for asking

- ✓ Do not use manipulative flattery to get what you want

- ✓ Explain why you are asking however do not over justify

- ✓ Be willing to accept a no

Examples of non-assertive requests:

'Is there any chance someone could move the boxes from the door, it's just that someone might complain about them being there.'

'I have got so much to do this week and I'm really worried that I'm not going to get the monthly return done. It would be great if someone else could pick it up.'

'I'm sorry to have to ask but I was wondering if there was any chance that you could babysit on Friday. I know it's a lot to ask so do say if you would rather not and I will try to find someone else.'

Rephrased as assertive requests:

'Will you please remove these boxes from the doorway as they are blocking the entrance?'

'I have agreed to do too many things this week and so wanted to know whether it is possible for you to do the monthly return?'

'I have been invited to a party on Friday and wanted to ask whether you would be able to babysit?'

2. Saying no

'No' – it is hard to believe that such a short word can be so difficult for us to say! In coaching and training sessions it is the thing that people identify most frequently as something that they need to work on. These are the reasons people give for now wanting to say no:

➢ 'I am worried about what people will think of me if I say no.'

➢ 'I might not be asked again.'

➢ 'I don't want people not to like me.'

➢ 'I am not sure if I have the right to say no.'

➢ 'I am afraid that I might get a hostile reaction.'

➢ 'I don't want people to think that I am unhelpful.'

➢ 'I hate upsetting people.'

It is important to recognise that we can make things worse by agreeing to do things that either we really don't want to do or don't have time to do. The negative consequences can be:

✗ We cancel things at short notice

✗ We fail to meet deadlines

✗ We get 'exploited' by other people

✗ We don't get the respect we deserve from other people

✗ We start to resent the people that are making the requests

✗ We don't do things as well as we can

✗ We begin to lose our self respect

✗ We spend time on other people's priorities rather than our own

One of the most common ways to avoid saying no is to make an excuse – have you ever told a white lie to avoid having to say no to someone?

Case study

Several years ago Moira attended an assertiveness course because she wanted to be able to say no more clearly – she explained to the group the situation that had caused her to sign up for the course. A colleague of hers had regularly been asking her for a lift home after work. Moira did not mind taking her occasionally but it was out of her way and added about 20 minutes to her journey. One Tuesday the colleague had said to her in the morning 'Can you take me home tonight?' Moira really didn't want to, however, she didn't want to upset or offend her so invented a reason why she couldn't take her home – she said ' I am sorry I can't tonight because I have got to go to the supermarket on my way home to do the shopping'. 'That's no problem' replied her colleague 'I could do with getting some things too so let's go shopping on the way back'.

Moira had ended up going to the supermarket and getting home an hour and a half later than she had planned! It was at that point that she decided the time had come to find a way to say no.

She worked on this example during the workshop and by the end had several different responses that she felt she would have been comfortable to use.

Option 1: 'I would prefer not to take you home tonight as it does take me out of my way and I would like to get straight back – however if there is anywhere that I can drop you along my route I am more than happy to do that.'

Option 2: 'I do need to get home on time tonight so I am afraid I won't be able to take you home.'

Option 3: 'I really do not mind taking you home occasionally however I will struggle to do it more than once a week.'

How to say no

There are two questions that you need to ask yourself when facing a situation that you don't want to say yes to:

➢ **Do I have the right to say no in this situation?**

➢ **If I do how can I do that in a way that is not aggressive or submissive?**

If you believe that you have the right then the following ideas may help you to exercise that right in an assertive way.

Here are three different ways to say no and choosing the most appropriate one is the first step.

A. The direct no

The direct no can feel quite abrupt and so many of us only feel comfortable using it if the request is very trivial e.g. 'Would you like a cup of coffee.' or if we believe the request is totally unreasonable e.g. 'Can I use your password to access these files?'. In both these cases most people feel that they can answer with a direct 'No.'

B. The flipping no

This involves refusing the request but making an alternative suggestion.

'Can you just show me how to do this before you go home?'
I do need to get home so cannot show you now, however I could come in early tomorrow morning to go through it – would that help?'

'Let's go out for dinner tonight'
I really don't feel like going out, how about getting a takeaway instead?'

C. The reasoned no

If we explain the reason that we cannot comply with the request it can make the refusal easier to make and easier for the other person to receive.

'Could you answer my phone for the next hour?
I am afraid I can't because I am going to a meeting in 15 minutes.'

'Would you like to come ten pin bowling with us tomorrow?'
'I appreciate you asking me however I really do not enjoy bowling and so will pass this time but thanks anyway.'

'Do you want to go for lunch later?'
'Thanks for the invitation however I cannot make it today as I have a report that has to be finished by 5.00pm.'

If you are going to use the reasoned no it is important that you are telling the truth and it is not just an excuse.

Also consider some of the things that you might have got in the habit of saying that undermine your no. It is often difficult to move away or change the subject, so we end by saying things like:

'Is that alright with you?'
'Do say if it is a problem.'
'Come back to me if you can't find anyone else.'
'I hope you won't think badly of me'

Once you have decided which sort of no you are going to use you also need to think about whether the word 'no' is going to be in the sentence. It is important that your message is clear however it is not always necessary to actually say no.

> **Case study**
>
> Many years ago I was in a library and observed a customer going to the desk and putting 4 books down on the counter and saying – 'Please could you be quick as I am in a real hurry.' The library assistant started to issue the books but found that the borrowers account had outstanding fines and so the account had been blocked. She looked up and said to the customer 'The computer is showing that your account currently has fines amounting to £10 so let me outline the options we have. You can pay the fines now by cash or cheque and then I can issue the books, you can pay 25% of the fine now and the rest when you return the books or I can hold the books for 24 hours and you can come back, pay the fines and take them – what would you like to do?' The lady decided to come back the next day and pay the fines and so asked for the books to be put to one side for 24 hours. At the end of the encounter she thanked the library assistant for being so helpful.

This was a perfect example of someone saying no without using the word. The library assistant was actually refusing to issue the books but rather than saying no you can't take them she focused the customers mind on what was possible rather than what wasn't.

If you are going to use the word 'no' in your response think about where it should be in the sentence. Starting with no can sound quite aggressive even if it isn't intended to – look at the example below.

'No I can't help with that even though I would like to.'

'I would like to help with that, however, I will have to say no.'

Exercise – Saying no

Look at the following examples and then plan your own.

The phone rings when you are eating your evening meal. You pick it up and the person on the other end says 'Good evening, I am ringing from a local window installation company with a once in a lifetime offer – how are you this evening?'

'This is not a convenient time as I am eating my evening meal. I do have a policy of not taking cold calls so please could you remove my details from your database.'

It is Monday morning and you have a mountain of things to do before your first meeting at 10.00am. A colleague arrives and pulls up a chair next to you and says 'Have you got a minute? I have got so much to tell you – you will never believe what happened to me this weekend.'

'I would love to hear what happened, however, I have loads to do before 10 o'clock so could we meet for lunch?'

Your manager has asked you to stay late – you had arranged to meet a friend for a drink and you don't want to cancel the arrangement.

....

....

....

....

Now think of a situation in which you find it hard to say no and answer the following questions.

Do you have the right to say no in this situation?

What do you worry will happen if you do say no?

How rational is that concern?

If you were going to say no how could you do it?

....
....
....
....
....
....
....
....
....
....

3. Raising an awkward issue

There are many conversations that we would like to have but do not know how to start them. The following model can help you to prepare what you want to say when raising an awkward issue with someone.

➢ **Introduce**

This is the explanation of the problem or situation, be specific and clear, ensure that you outline the facts not your interpretation of them. It is important that the issue is described in as neutral a way as possible. If you start to attribute blame the other person is likely to become defensive quite quickly

➢ **Impact**

This involves describing what is happening as a result of the above. This may mean explaining how the situation is making you feel or the effect something is having on the service or wider organisation.

➢ **Discuss**

The third part of the model involves discussing what action could be taken to address the issue. Take the time to explore the other person's point of view. Do be clear, direct and realistic about what you would like to happen however do leave room for negotiation.

Here are a few examples of the model in practice.

Nick (manager) to Maggie (member of staff)

Introduce: Maggie, I would like to talk to you about the use of Facebook in the office. At the team meeting in January we agreed that staff would only access their Facebook during their lunch hour and yet on at least three occasions today when I have passed your desk Facebook has been on your screen.

Impact: I am concerned that it may be affecting your work as well as setting a poor example to other members of the team.

Discuss: Is there any reason why you are not following the procedure that we agreed?

Gaynor (manager) to Samir (member of staff)

Introduce: Samir I want to talk to you about your timekeeping. In the last fortnight you have arrived over 20 minutes late on four occasions.

Impact: This has meant that someone else has had to open the reception desk for you and deal with enquiries. It is not fair on other staff as they all have their own work to do in the morning.

Discuss: How can we prevent this happening in the future?

Sally to Freya (friends)

Introduce: A couple of times recently you have borrowed clothes to wear on nights out and then not returned them to me for several weeks.

Impact: This has meant that on a few occasions I have wanted to wear something and it hasn't been in my wardrobe.

Discuss: I am really happy to continue to lend things to you but could we agree that you will return them within a week?

We avoid raising issues because we make assumptions about what other people are thinking and often we get it wrong.

Case study

Darren and Mia had started to dread Christmas. They had been married for five years – the year after they had married they had wanted to see both sets of parents on Christmas Day so had gone to Darren's parents for lunch and then driven 50 miles to have tea with Mia's parents. They did not want to upset either family and so had continued to do this for the next four years. They both felt that Christmas was being compromised because they did not relax all day and both families complained that their visit was too short. Despite this neither of them felt they could have the conversation with their parents about doing things differently c of them. It was beginning to create tension between Darren and Mia so they decided to raise the issue with both families. They introduced the issue by explaining why they had been visiting both families. They then outlined the impact and suggested that it would be far more enjoyable if they could spend the whole day and evening with them rather than rushing away. They suggested coming to them on alternate Christmas Days and spending Boxing Day with the other family. Darren's mother said 'I am surprised that you haven't suggested it before, I always thought it was daft to drive all that way but I didn't want to say anything in case it offended you.' Mia's family were happy with the new arrangement and Christmas became a far more relaxed and enjoyable time for everyone.

*'When you spend your life worrying about how other people feel:
you lose track of how you feel.'*

4. Disagreeing with someone

When someone says something that we disagree with it is understandable that our instinctive reaction is to tell them why they are wrong. Clearly if the issue is a very factual one and you know and have the evidence to support your view it may be appropriate to explain it. However, in many cases it is not that clear cut and using the PACE technique helps you stop and think about their viewpoint before jumping in with yours – try using this before responding.

> **Pause –** do not respond immediately, count to 10 before saying anything in order to let your instinctive response pass.

> **Ask Questions –** use insightful questions to help you understand their side of the argument – some examples are:

> 'Tell me more about.....'
> 'Can you give me an example?'
> 'Can you help me to understand that viewpoint?'
> 'I had never thought of it like that, could you give me a bit more detail?'
> 'Can you talk me through how you reached that conclusion?'

> **Choose –** decide whether the new information means that you want to change your viewpoint.

> **Engage –** respond

Tips for responding:

> Do not push your case too forcibly – just repeating the same thing over and over again will raise resistance in the other person,

> Try to avoid using verbal irritators such as 'With all due respect' or 'I think you will find' or 'Let's be honest here.'

> Do not use language that is patronising e.g. 'What you don't seem to have grasped here is....' or 'If you would listen to me for more than 30 seconds...' or 'Look I don't want to argue with you, but.........'

> Use positive language:

'I think we may have different views on this, can I tell you how I see it'

'I do not believe that all staff are demotivated'

I do not agree with all the points that you have made although I appreciate you being honest about how you feel.'

'I recognise that we have not had the same experience, however, I would like to share my experience with you..........'

When we disagree with someone we have a tendency to focus on the difference. We invest a lot of energy in restating our own view in order to get someone to agree. The interaction is likely to be more productive if we use that energy to focus on how the situation can be resolved.

5. Handling angry people

There are three key stages in dealing with someone that is angry.

➢ Stage 1 – Calming

➢ Stage 2 – Reaching

➢ Stage 3 – Moving Forward

Situations are often unintentionally escalated because people do not realise the importance of following this sequence. There is no point in trying to reason with someone who is angry – until the strong emotion has passed the individual will be unlikely to be listening and therefore trying to have a rational conversation is pointless. It is important that these three stages are not seen as being completely discrete, each one is dependent on the others. The chances of successfully resolving an aggressive encounter come from flexibility in returning to a previous stage of the trilogy if progress is hindered.

Whatever you say or do it must be done with feeling and sincerity, if you sound patronising or bored, you will exacerbate the situation.

Stage 1 – Calming

➢ Display calmness – although this can be very hard it is important that you never lose your own temper as this will only add fuel to the fire. It is much harder for the other person to remain angry if you are obviously not responding in the same way.

➢ Encourage the other person to talk – an angry person will run out of steam, usually in under two minutes, if nothing is done to aggravate the situation. Use non-verbal prompts to encourage him or her to talk. Listen carefully and gather as much information as you can – resist the urge at this stage to counter arguments or disagree.

➢ Avoid an audience – don't allow the other person to play 'to the gallery'. The audience may be drawn to take sides or increase the likelihood of a loss of face. Often the act of walking to another room can begin to calm someone down.

➢ Take your time – create the space to deal with the situation. If the other person senses that you are impatient to finish the encounter they will become increasingly agitated and it may well lengthen the time it takes to calm them down.

Note of caution: although the best way to deal with anger in someone else is to listen and let them calm down, that does not mean anyone has the right to use inappropriate language or treat you abusively. If at any point, you feel that they have stepped over that boundary, you need to stop the conversation with a clear and assertive statement, I would usually put my hand up and say something like:

'I am very willing to have this conversation however I am not willing to be spoken to like that.' or

'I am happy to discuss your complaint although I will end the conversation if you continue to make personal comments.' or

'I would like to resolve this however I am not prepared to be sworn at.'

Stage 2 – Reaching

Once the initial anger seems to have passed you need to demonstrate that you have listened and understood their position. This is not to say that you necessarily agree with it but you do need show that you can summarise the key points they are making. Often when someone is angry all their grievances pour out, try to identify each issue and summarise them individually. You may also need to ask some clarifying questions – be careful that you do not appear to be judging as this could reignite the anger.

'Can I check that I have understood this correctly...........'

'You seem to be saying.......................is that right?'

'Can I clarify a couple of points.................?'

'So my understanding is that............................have I missed anything?'

Once the other person has accepted that your summary is accurate they will be ready to move to the final stage.

Stage 3 – Moving forward

This is the point at which you can begin to voice your point of view. This may involve offering an alternative perspective or replying factually to the issues that have been raised. It may be appropriate to use questions to move the situation forward.

Some examples include:

'How would you like to see this progress from here?'

'What do you think our options are?'

'What are you hoping that I will be able to do?'

'That decision has been made so how do you feel we can move forward from here?'

'I am not sure that we are going to agree on this so can you think of a resolution that we can both live with?'

6. Being put on the spot

There are many occasions when someone asks or says something and our immediate reaction is one of panic because we don't know how to respond. A key skill of assertive behaviour is not allowing yourself to be hijacked because, when we are, we often respond in a way that we later regret – it is far better to take 'time out' to decide the most appropriate way to deal with the situation.

When we are put on the spot our instinctive responses tend to be fight or flight ones. These are instant reactions that have no cognitive thought associated with them – finding ways to allow time for rational thinking is crucial. This is important because this instinctive fight or flight response is part of our survival mechanism and so will always be the first thing to kick in. In most day to day situations your life isn't at stake and so responding instinctively is not necessarily the best course of action.

Practise time out phrases to use next time someone puts you on the spot:

'I will check my diary for next week and see if that is possible – I will ring you back in 5 minutes.'

'I will need a minute to think about that.'

'That's not a possibility I had considered – I will give it some thought and get back to you tomorrow.'

'Thanks for the invitation, I will speak to ……. and get back to you this evening.'

'I think this is something that deserves more attention – can we arrange a more convenient time to talk about it?'

7. Standing your ground

The following case study demonstrates a technique called the broken record. This can be useful if you feel that your message is being ignored or dismissed. In essence it is about remaining focused on the key issue that you want to discuss and not allowing side issues or deviations to get in the way.

Case study

Ahmed and Jane are colleagues who are jointly responsible for producing a weekly e-mail bulletin for their department. For the last few weeks Ahmed has done it on his own because Jane has said that she has been too busy.

The bulletin is due out tomorrow and Ahmed has an urgent report to finish by the end of the day.

Ahmed: Jane, would you be able to do the bulletin this week as I have an urgent report to finish by the end of today.

Jane: Sorry, absolutely no way – I am up to my eyes in work.

Ahmed: I have done it for the last few weeks and it is a joint responsibility.

Jane: It's not my fault that I have a lot to do, can't you just do it once more, it doesn't take much time

Ahmed: I cannot complete my report and get the bulletin out by the end of today.

Jane: Well it is ridiculously short notice, you could have let me know earlier that you were going to have a problem

Ahmed: I appreciate it is short notice however I did not know until yesterday that the report would be asked for and I can only do the report or the bulletin.

Jane: How urgent is the report?

Ahmed: I have to give it to the Director by 5.00pm tonight.

Jane: OK well leave the bulletin with me and I will see what I can do.

In this example Ahmed does not allow Jane's low level aggression to affect his behaviour. He remains assertive and keeps returning to the reason for having the conversation.

Examples of broken record in practice:

It is Monday and your friend has rung to ask you to go to the cinema with her tomorrow evening, you have told her on a few occasions that Tuesday is not a convenient night.

'I would like to go to the cinema with you although I cannot go tomorrow. Tuesday is never a good night for me because my partner is at an evening class. I can do most nights of the week however Tuesdays are rarely going to be possible.'

Your manager asked you an hour ago for some figures – you told her it would take about three hours to do them and she has already asked you twice if they are ready. She has just come in again and said 'Haven't you finished those yet?'

'My original estimate of 3 hours was pretty accurate and so I won't be able to complete them before 5.00pm. If there are some areas that are more urgent than others I can do those first and get them to you however the rest will take three hours.'

8. Handling put downs

Put downs are remarks that are designed to make you feel small or coerce you into doing something that you don't want to do. They are usually sarcastic, belittling or patronising

This type of behaviour is aggressive and you need to recognise it as such because otherwise it can leave you feeling quite confused. It is the type of behaviour that we respond to instinctively i.e. fight or flight and then regret. The best way to deal with it is to ignore the manner in which the remark has been made and answer it honestly and truthfully.

The following are examples of the type of put downs you may have heard or experienced and some possible responses:

'Well if I were you I wouldn't put up with it, I would tell him straight.'
'Thank you for your suggestion and I will bear it in mind when I am deciding how to deal with it.'

'That's just typical of a woman.'
'I don't know if it is typical of all women however it is my opinion'

'Correct me if I am wrong but I think you will find.....'
'It is not a question of right or wrong, I do believe the best way forward is....'

'Come off it, you know as well as I do that it didn't happen like that.'
'It is the way that I saw it.'

'Don't be so touchy about it; he talks to everyone like that, don't worry about it.'
'I am worried about it as I don't think the fact that he does it to everyone is a good enough reason.'

'The trouble with you is you take everything so seriously – lighten up it was only a bit of fun.'
'This is not a question of lightening up, I do think sexist remarks are a serious issue.'

9. Responding to criticism

It is never easy to receive criticism and once again our instinctive response is to defend. Emotionally we want to either kick back or run away and hide. Therefore the first stage in dealing with criticism is to take a deep breath and then decide whether you feel that the criticism is valid or not.

If there is some truth in what has been said then:

➢ Acknowledge all or part of your responsibility
➢ Apologise if appropriate
➢ Focus on what you can do to improve

'I did forget to send that e-mail yesterday and I am really sorry. I would be very willing to ring the supplier and apologise directly.'
'Yes I think you are right, I was quite abrupt yesterday and I am sorry if I hurt your feelings, I didn't mean to.'
'I recognise that my time keeping has not been as good as it should have been recently and I am going to ensure that it improves.'

If you believe the criticism is not valid:

➢ Outline your reasons for not agreeing with the comment
➢ Ask for an explanation

'I did send the e-mail before I left last night; I have checked and there is a copy in my sent folder.'
'I was not aware that I was rude and abrupt yesterday – would it be possible to outline what made it feel like that?'
'I have only been late one morning this month – do you think it has been more than that?'

If the criticism is non-specific:

➢ Ask for more details

'You really do need to improve your report writing.'
Could you tell me which bits you think need more work?'
'Well they do go on a bit and your grammar isn't great.'
'Please could you go through my last report and highlight the areas that you feel could be improved – I would really appreciate it.'

10. Dealing with negativity

It can be very tiring working, or socialising, with someone who constantly has a negative response to anything that happens. In my experience this can be for a number of different reasons:

Some people are genetically more pessimistic than others.

Sometimes an individual has had bad experiences in the past that have made them start to assume the worst in all situations.

Negativity can become a habit and the individual does not even realise that they are doing it.

Some people enjoy moaning – I remember a course delegate once saying 'My parents don't really enjoy an evening out if everything goes well because then they don't have anything to talk about!'

It can also be that the person believes that they are being helpful by always pointing out the possible risks or downsides of a situation.

There is no magic answer to dealing with negativity. It is important to ensure the focus is on reality, acknowledge the any truth in what they are saying (if there is any) and ask for ideas for improvement.

Examples:
'You are right, I think it is going to be a difficult transition to make. What do you think would make it easier?'
'I can see that it will be odd having to share an office after all this time – what do you think you can do to help you adapt?'

If the behaviour is a repeating pattern it is often valuable to highlight to someone their tendency not to contribute positively.

Examples:
'I have heard you mention on a number of occasions that you don't like working here, are there any aspects of the job or the organisation that you do like.'
'It would be good to hear something positive from you.'

11. Receiving compliments

Many people find receiving compliments an area that is difficult to handle.

Do any of the following exchanges sound familiar?

'I like your dress it really suits you.'
'Thanks – it was only cheap, I got it on the market for £10.'

'I wanted to thank you for all the work you did organising the conference last week – it went so well.'
'Really it was nothing, anyone could have done it.'

'I have bought these flowers to thank you for the lovely meal you cooked for us on Saturday.'
'Thank you but you really shouldn't have bothered.'

'Weren't your children beautifully behaved during the show – it was a long time for them to sit so quietly.'
'You wouldn't have said that if you could have seen them at 6.00 o'clock this morning.'

These represent some of the most common ways that people deflect compliments by either putting themselves or others down or by minimising what has been said. Start to notice the way that you respond when someone says something positive to you.

How easy do you find it to say thank you and NOTHING else?

If someone has taken the time to pay the compliment we have the responsibility to accept it is meant and receive it graciously.

12. Giving feedback

If you were doing something that was really annoying or upsetting someone would you want to know? If you were doing something that other people thought was really good would you want to know? Generally people will answer yes to both of these questions and yet we are often reticent about giving feedback to other people.

Feedback is information about someone's behaviour that we share in order to affirm or change what they do.

Feedback is really valuable and helps us all to become more aware of our behaviour and the effect it has on others however it is imperative that it is given in a constructive way.

A checklist for giving constructive feedback

✓ Focus on the behaviour not on the person

✓ Describe the behaviour but do not evaluate it or make judgements

✓ Use 'I' statements to accept responsibility for your own perceptions

✓ Be specific not general

✓ Share ideas and information rather than giving advice. Use words like 'I thought' or 'I felt' not 'You ought' or 'You should'

✓ Ensure the timing is appropriate

The BED model

Using the **BED** model of feedback can help to ensure that your feedback is well structured.

> **B – Behaviour:** Describe the behaviour in a non-judgemental way – give examples of what you have seen or heard

> **E – Effect:** Describe clearly the effect or impact the behaviour is having – if positive, thank and close

> **D – Discuss:** Ask a question to invite a response to the feedback

Examples of the BED Model in practice:

B – A couple of times this week I have said good morning to you and you haven't replied

E – When that happens I worry that I have done something to upset or offend you

D – Is there any reason why you don't always reply?

B – The report that you gave me yesterday on the office move had a really clear summary at the beginning

E- I found that made it really easy to understand and I wanted to thank you.

B – Every day this week I have come home to a sink full of dirty dishes

E – I find It really difficult not to get snappy because it makes me feel as though you all wait for me to get home to do the clearing up

D – Can we manage this differently?

B – Every morning when I walk in you smile and ask how I am

E – It always makes me feel good – thank you.

Exercise – Choosing the technique

Look at the following scenarios and decide which technique you would use if you wanted to handle the situation assertively.

1. On a night out a few weeks ago you lent a friend £20 and she still hasn't paid you back. You have seen her several times and have dropped a few hints about feeling a bit short of money but she has not offered to return the money.

....

....

....

....

2. A colleague wants your help with a non-urgent matter. You are happy to help however not at the moment as you want to finish a report before you go home.

....

....

....

....

3. You are looking for a present for a friend and the sales assistant has gone to a lot of trouble finding a range of things for you to look at, however, you are not sure if they are exactly what you want.

....

....

....

....

4. It is Monday morning and you have a mountain of things to do before your first meeting at 10.00am. A colleague arrives and pulls up a chair next to you and says, 'Have you got a minute? I have got so much to tell you – you will never believe what happened to me this weekend.'

....

....

....

....

5. You are out with a group of your partner's friends who you do not know particularly well. One of them begins to say some quite unpleasant and, in your opinion, untrue things about a close friend of yours.

....

....

....

....

6. Over the last few weeks your colleague has been taking a lot of personal calls during working hours. As a consequence you are doing quite a lot of extra work to ensure things get done, you are beginning to feel quite annoyed that she is expecting you to fill in for her.

....

....

....

....

7. Weeks ago you agreed to a sales person giving you a quote for some new windows in your house. You have decided that you can't afford them at the moment but said that you may come back to the company next year if your financial position improves. Since then you have received several phone calls from the company which have been attempts to get you to agree to have the work done in six months time.

....

....

....

....

8. You have forgotten to do something that your manager told you was urgent. The next day she asks to see you and says 'That was a really serious mistake and I do feel you need to improve your attitude to work.'

....

....

....

....

Some suggestions for ideas on how to deal with these scenarios can be found at the end of the book.

Chapter Five:
Putting it into Practice

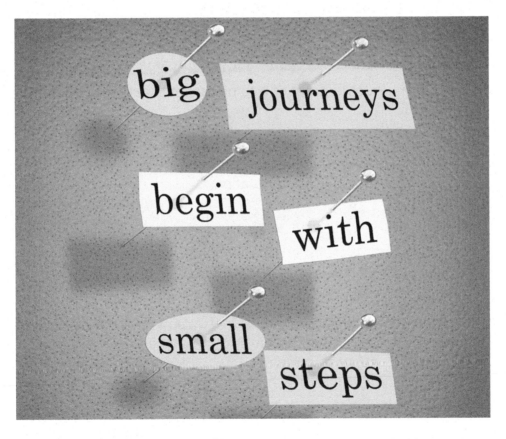

'Knowledge is of no value unless you put
it into practice.' Anton Chekhov

Chapter Five:
Putting it into Practice

This chapter will help you to:

✓ Understand the assertiveness cycle

✓ Decide what you want the outcome of a situation to be

✓ Practise preparing to be assertive in specific situations

There are 4 stages in the assertiveness cycle. These are the questions you need to ask yourself when preparing to be assertive in a given situation.

What do I want
to happen?

Do I have the confidence to
address this issue?
What are my fears?

How can I deal
with this assertively?

Am I willing and able
to listen and compromise
about this issue?

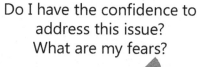

Stage 1: What do I want to happen?

Assertive behaviour begins with being clear about what a successful outcome looks like – this is critical because if we don't know what we want how can we expect anyone else to know? This may sound very obvious but think about the number of times you have heard people complaining about a situation and being very clear about what they DON'T want or are unhappy about but a lot less clear about what they do want. The following two cases are examples of this in practice.

Case study

Several years ago one of my children opened a present on Christmas morning that was broken, she was really upset and as parents we felt a mixture of anger (with the store for selling a faulty item) and guilt (for not having checked before wrapping the present). The following day I stormed into the shop to complain about the fact that our Christmas day had been marred by this event. I spent several minutes explaining how disappointed I was and that I expected more from somewhere that was a household name. When I had finished the assistant acknowledged how frustrating the experience must have been and then asked very politely. 'How would you like to see this progress from here?' In that one question she completely floored me – what did I want? 'Well I would like the item replacing' I replied. 'That is no problem madam, I will get another one and ensure that it is in full working order before you leave the shop' – clearly this was not enough, I was still angry and quite upset but what did I want? In my frustration I said 'Well I have had the inconvenience of having to trail back here today and so I would like my petrol money reimbursing' 'That is no problem – if you can let me know how far you have travelled I can arrange a refund.' At this point I began to feel increasingly uneasy – did I really want £2.80 for petrol money? Would that make it alright?' No, because what I really wanted was for it not to have happened and that wasn't possible.

Case study

Sarah had just been in a meeting with a range of people from across her organisation. She was presenting some ideas that she had been working on for several months when her manager (who was chairing the meeting) suddenly announced in a strident voice 'I am going to stop you there Sarah because several of these figures are incorrect and you need to check them before we consider this proposal. I would like us to move on to the next item on the agenda.' Sarah was extremely embarrassed and incredibly angry.

I met her straight after the meeting, she looked upset and so I asked her if she was OK.

'No' she replied 'I am livid, Charlotte has just completely humiliated me in front of half of the senior management team and I am on my way to ask her what on earth she thought she was doing.'

'What do you want the conversation to achieve?' I asked.

'I want her to know how I feel about what she did.'

'OK so you want her to understand that you were upset and embarrassed – is that all you want?'

'No, I want her to acknowledge that she was wrong and that the figures are correct – I spent ages putting them together and she dismissed them.'

'Right so if she recognises how you feel and acknowledges that the figures are the right ones will you feel better?'

'Partly, but I also want her to apologise in an e-mail to all the other people that were at the meeting and tell them that the figures are right and rearrange the meeting........'

At this point she sat down and said 'I think I really need to prepare for this conversation.' We went for a coffee and worked out exactly what she hoped the conversation with Charlotte would achieve.

These two case studies demonstrate some of the traps we fall into:

➢ Sometimes we react emotionally to situations and don't stop to think, what do I hope to achieve here and how realistic is that?

➢ Often we frame what we want in terms of changing the other person

> 'I want him to be more thoughtful'
> 'I want her to understand me better'

These are unlikely to be achievable because we have little control over other people

➢ We can state what we don't want but can struggle to turn that into something we do want

➢ We forget to stop and ask ourselves what the other person might be thinking

➢ We can be very vague about our wants and this can cause confusion often resulting in misunderstandings

*'If you don't know where you are going
you will probably end up somewhere else' Laurence Peter*

Stage 2: Do I have the confidence to address this issue? What are my fears?

If you are going to become more assertive you will need to step out of your comfort zone. However, it is really important that those steps are small to begin with. Therefore it is critical to ask yourself these questions before going any further. If the answer is that you do not feel you have the confidence then look back at the confidence building ideas in chapter 2. Is there anything you could do to help develop your confidence to deal with this situation?

Stage 3: How can I deal with this assertively?

Deciding the best way to communicate is another important element of your preparation. As well as the skills and techniques covered in earlier chapters there are a number of other things to consider:

➢ Which method of communication should I use?
There are lots of ways to communicate today- text, email, phone, video conference, face to face etc. If there is any emotional content to the issue you are dealing with then face to face communication is usually the most effective. Misunderstandings are highly prevalent in leaner forms of communication such as email and text.

➢ What is the right time and place to have this conversation?

➢ Write a plan which covers what you want to say. This is not a script but it will help you to clarify your thinking.

➢ Rehearse out loud! Speaking aloud is very different to running something through you mind. You will 'hear' things differently.

➢ Make sure you practise enough so that what you want to say is firmly in your mind.

Stage 4: Am I willing and able to listen and compromise about this issue?

Remember true assertiveness is about the right to state your view and opinion as well as the responsibility to listen and accept that someone else may have a different viewpoint.

The following scenarios are based on this 4 stage approach. Have a look at them and then use a real example from your life to use the process.

Scenario one – Sam's story

Sam has recently been appointed as the manager of a small administrative team. During his first month he has noticed that the atmosphere in the office is really positive, morale in the team is high, everyone seems motivated and working hard. However, he has also noticed that all the members of the team come to his office to ask or check things with him before taking any action - this results in people asking him things 30 – 40 times day. He would like staff to be able to take more responsibility for their own work and not feel that everything has to be run past him.

Sam's preparation

What do I want to happen?

I would like people to have the confidence to deal with things without feeling that they have to check them with me.

Do I have the confidence to address this issue? What are my concerns?

I do want to address the issue and believe that I have the confidence to do it. However I do not what to adversely affect the morale of the team. My main concern is that people will think that I am being dictatorial, that I am unapproachable and I do not want that to happen.

How can I deal with this assertively?

I would like to develop a system of communication that still provides support to all the staff but in a more systematic way. I am therefore going to suggest implementing regular one to one meetings with all my staff and ask them to bring non urgent matters to those meetings. I will introduce the idea at the next team meeting – this is what I am going to say:

'I am conscious that you all have things that you need to discuss with me and sometimes when this is done in an ad hoc way I worry that I am not giving each matter the undivided attention it deserves. Therefore, what I would like to suggest is that we arrange for each of you to have a weekly half hour one to one meeting with me in which to ask any questions, raise concerns or discuss problems. How does that sound?'

Am I willing and able to listen and compromise?

I definitely want to hear the teams views about this so will allow time for discussion at the meeting but will also suggest that we trial the new system for a few weeks and then discuss it again.

Scenario two – Amelia's story

Amelia has been living away from home for the last two years at University. When she comes home during the holidays her mother assumes that she will babysit for her younger sister Emma so that she can go out. Alison doesn't mind doing it at all but it annoys her that her mother doesn't check that she is free to babysit before making her arrangements. Earlier in the week Alison had to cancel a planned trip to the cinema because her mother was going out.

Amelia's preparation

What do I want to happen?

I would like Mum to check with me before she makes arrangements that require me to babysit.

Do I have the confidence to address this issue?
What are my concerns?

I do not want Mum or Emma to think that I do not want to babysit as I am really happy to do it but I do want to address the issue because I don't think it is fair.

How can I deal with this assertively?

I need to have a chat with Mum and explain how I feel and this is how I am going to open the conversation:

'Mum, on a couple of occasions since I have come home you have arranged to go out and have then told me that I am babysitting for Emma. I am very happy to look after her. However, I do find it frustrating that you don't check with me first. Could we put a calendar on the fridge and put our plans on it so that we can check each other's availability before making arrangements?'

Am I willing and able to listen and compromise?

Provided that Mum understands my point of view I am very willing to discuss how we manage the situation differently.

Scenario three – Cassie's story

Cassie has recently moved to a new job. She used to work in the same organisation but for a different department. In her last job she had an annual appraisal in which her training needs for the year were discussed and agreed. Her new manager has said that she doesn't believe in the appraisal process as she thinks it is better to have conversations as and when they are needed and not at a time decided by HR. Cassie would like to have a conversation with her new manager about her training for the next year but every time she raises the issue her manager says 'There is no rush for that you have only just started with us.'

Cassie's preparation

What do I want to happen?

I would like to sit down with my manager and discuss my personal development.

Do I have the confidence to address this issue? What are my concerns?

I have tried to approach her face to face and have been dismissed so I do not feel confident about trying that again but I do not want to let the issue go because it is really important to me as I want to develop and progress.

What advice would you give Cassie on how to deal with this situation assertively?

....

....

....

....

....

Scenario four – Your story

What do I want to happen?

....
....
....
....
....
....
....
....
....
....

Do I have the confidence to address this issue?
What are my fears?

....
....
....
....
....
....
....
....
....
....
....
....

How can I deal with this assertively?

....

....

....

....

....

....

....

....

Am I willing and able to listen and compromise about this issue?

....

....

....

....

....

....

....

....

....

....

Chapter 6:
Action Planning

'Nobody trips over mountains. It is the small pebble that causes you to stumble. Pass all the pebbles in your path and you will find you have crossed the mountain.'

Chapter Six:
Action Planning

Please pick up a pen and write your name in the box below using the hand that you do not usually write with.

```



```

How did that feel? Probably quite awkward and clumsy and so next time you pick up a pen you are likely to go back to using the hand that you always write with (unless you have broken your arm!). It is quicker and more comfortable and this highlights the dilemma with a lot of learning, it involves time, practise and patience.

If you have read this book it is probably because you want to do something differently and therefore I hope you are willing to invest the time that will be needed to make those changes. If you start to get frustrated remember developing new skills is not always easy.

The conscious competence ladder shows how we move through four different stages when learning something new. This model can help you to understand and manage your emotions during that process.

The conscious competence ladder

Unconscious competence

Conscious competence

Conscious incompetence

Unconscious incompetence

> ➤ **Level 1: Unconscious incompetence**
> **We don't know what we don't know**

This is the level at which we are either unaware of the need for the skill or do not see the relevance or usefulness to us.

> ➤ **Level 2: Conscious incompetence**
> **You know that you don't know**

At this point we become aware of how much we do not know. Do you remember your first driving lesson? Many people will say that they felt completely overwhelmed with how much they needed to learn and remember thinking 'I will never be able to do all this.' This stage of learning can be quite uncomfortable and sometimes people wish that they hadn't begun and may even give up. If, however, you persevere you move into conscious competence.

> ➤ **Level 3: Conscious competence**
> **You know that you know**

This is the stage at which we are beginning to master the skill but still need to think about it. So with driving this was the time that you were mentally saying to yourself 'Put the key in the ignition, start the car, put my foot on the clutch, check all mirrors etc.' This step of the ladder often feels quite clunky. You are doing things differently but it does not feel easy or natural. After a while the internal dialogue stops and we move to level 4.

> **Level 4: Unconscious competence**
> **You don't think about what you know**

This is when the new behaviour has become something that you do without thinking, it becomes second nature. The day you drive to work without remembering the journey,

So you need to identify small changes that you want to make and record them on the action plan. Do not set yourself really difficult or challenging goals because as with any good training you need to build your muscles up gradually.

And remember:

'If you always do what you have always done,
you will always get what you have always got.'

Personal action plan

The purpose of this action plan is to identify areas that you want to work on and decide what action you are going to take. Look back through the exercises in the book to help you.

'The great end of learning is not knowledge but action.' Peter Honey

Example action plan:

Area to work on	Action
Receiving compliments	Next time someone compliments me I will say thank you and nothing else.
Avoiding snapping at my mother in law	Develop a 'banked phrase' to use when she comments on the way that I am bringing up the children.
Developing my self-confidence	Borrow 'Feel the fear and do it anyway' from the library.
Understand what assertive behaviour looks like	Look for role models at work and notice how they behave.

My action plan

Area to work on	Action

Final thoughts

One thing I have learned over the last 25 years is that developing a strong communication capability is a journey and no-one has completed it. This is what makes it so interesting, human behaviour is fascinating and people never fail to surprise me. I hope this book has helped you on your path to becoming a more confident communicator and if there is anything you would like to comment on or discuss please do contact me.

There are a few final thoughts that I would like to leave you with:

If you are going to grow and develop you will have to be willing to step out of your comfort zone. Please ensure that these steps are small to begin with to allow time for your confidence and capability to grow. Remember good learning takes time, practise and patience.

Start to observe the way other people behave and look for positive role models. If I hear someone dealing with a situation really well I will often jot down some of the key phrases or words that they have used.

Things will not always go the way you want them to and when that happens reflect on what went wrong, learn from your mistakes and then move on and on the occasions that you get it right remember to congratulate yourself!

Good luck and Best Wishes

Deborah

Further Reading

The Self Esteem Workbook by Lynda Field
978-1852306458

Feel the Fear and Do It Anyway by Susan Jeffers
978-0091907075

How to Change Absolutely Anything by Damian Hughes
978-0273770916

Assertiveness at Work by Ken Back and Kate Back
978-0077114282

Difficult Conversations by Anne Dickson
978-0749926755

Vital Conversations by Alec Grimsley
978-0956312808

Put Emotional Intelligence to Work
by Jeff Feldman and Karl Mulle
978-1562864828

Ideas for the exercise at the end of chapter 4

1. On a night out a few weeks ago you lent a friend £20 and she still hasn't paid you back. You have seen her several times and have dropped a few hints about feeling a bit short of money but she has not offered to return the money.

This requires a direct request to be made for the money. 'Hi, I am not sure if you remember but when we were shopping in town you borrowed £20 from me – please could I have it back?'

2. A colleague wants your help with a non-urgent matter. You are happy to help however not at the moment as you want to finish a report before you go home.

I would suggest using a flipping no in this situation. You do want to help your colleague however it is not convenient to do so now. 'I am more than happy to go through that with you. I have to finish this report today so how about we meet first thing tomorrow morning?'

3. You are looking for a present for a friend and the sales assistant has gone to a lot of trouble finding a range of things for you to look at, however, you are not sure if they are exactly what you want.

I would recommend using a time out phrase in this situation. 'Thank you very much for your help I really appreciate it. I need to go away and think about what you have shown me and make a decision.'

4. It is Monday morning and you have a mountain of things to do before your first meeting at 10.00am. A colleague arrives and pulls up a chair next to you and says, 'Have you got a minute? I have got so much to tell you – you will never believe what happened to me this weekend'.

A combination of a reasoned and flipping no is probably the easiest way to deal with this – 'I can't wait to hear however I do have to finish this before 10.00am so how about we meet for lunch?'

5. You are out with a group of your partner's friends who you do not know particularly well. One of them begins to say some quite unpleasant and, in your opinion, untrue things about a close friend of yours.

In this scenario you want to support your friend but at the same time do not want to create tension in a social situation. Therefore stating your opinion in a clear way without contradicting the other person is one way to deal with this assertively. 'I have known Kate for quite a long time and that has not been my experience of her, she has always been very honest and reliable in her dealings with me.'

6. Over the last few weeks your colleague has been taking a lot of personal calls during working hours. As a consequence you are doing quite a lot of extra work to ensure things get done, you are beginning to feel quite annoyed that she is expecting you to fill in for her.

The risk with this situation is that you start to get annoyed and make assumptions about the other person's behaviour before discussing it with them. The earlier you tackle this the better so use the introduce, impact, discuss model to raise the issue with them. 'There have been quite a few occasions this week when I have had to deal with queries at the desk because you have been on the phone. I have noticed that you have been receiving a lot more personal calls than usual – is everything alright?'

7. Weeks ago you agreed to a sales person giving you a quote for some new windows in your house. You have decided that you can't afford them at the moment but said that you may come back to the company next year if your financial position improves. Since then you have received several phone calls from the company which have been attempts to get you to agree to have the work done in six months time.

In this type of situation we often feel slightly awkward because we did agree to the quote being done in the first place. It is important to remember that you have the right to say no and to change your mind. I would therefore recommend using broken record – 'As I told your colleague when he rang last week I do not want to commit to this work at the moment. If I do decide to have the work done I will contact you but I would like to stress that I do not want to sign up to anything now and I do not want to receive any further phone calls regarding this quote. If I decide that I want to have the work done I will ring you.'

8. You have forgotten to do something that your manager told you was urgent. The next day she asks to see you and says 'That was a really serious mistake and I do feel you need to improve your attitude to work.'

In a situation like this it is important to acknowledge the mistake and apologise for it. The second part of the comment is not specific and therefore requires clarification so that you can decide whether there is any truth in it. 'I am really sorry that I forgot to do that and I will make sure that I do it this morning. I was not aware that you were generally unhappy with my attitude to work and I would appreciate the opportunity to hear your concerns – could we meet again this afternoon?'

Notes:

Universe of Learning Books

"The purpose of learning is growth, and our minds, unlike our bodies, can continue growing as we continue to live." Mortimer Adler

About the publishers

Universe of Learning Limited is a small publisher based in the UK with production in England, Australia and America. Our authors are all experienced trainers or teachers who have taught their skills for many years. We are actively seeking qualified authors and if you visit the authors section on www.uolearn.com you can find out how to apply.

If you are interested in any of our current authors (including Deborah Dalley) coming to speak at your event please do visit their own websites (to contact Deborah please email deborah@uolearn.com, website www.deborahdalley.com) or email them through the author section of the uolearn site.

If you would like to purchase larger numbers of books then please do contact us (sales@uolearn.com). We give discounts from 5 books upwards. For larger volumes we can also quote for changes to the cover to accommodate your company logo and to the interior to brand it for your company.

All our books are written by teachers, trainers or people well experienced in their roles and our goal is to help people develop their skills with a well structured range of exercises.

If you have any feedback about this book or other topics that you'd like to see us cover please do contact us at support@uolearn.com.

To buy the printed books please order from your favourite bookshop, including Amazon, Waterstones, Blackwells and Barnes and Noble. For ebooks please visit www.uolearn.com.

Keep Learning!

Developing Your Influencing Skills

ISBN: 978-1-84937-004-2, from www.uolearn.com
- ✓ Decide what your influencing goals are
- ✓ Find ways to increase your credibility rating
- ✓ Develop stronger and more trusting relationships
- ✓ Inspire others to follow your lead
- ✓ Become a more influential communicator

Packed with case studies, exercises and practical tips to become more influential.

Report Writing

An easy to follow format for writing reports

ISBN 978-1-84937-036-3, from www.uolearn.com

This book makes report writing a step by step process for you to follow every time you have a report to write.

- ✓ How to set objectives using 8 simple questions
- ✓ Easy to follow flow chart
- ✓ How to write an executive summary
- ✓ How to layout and structure the report
- ✓ Help people remember what they read

Stress Management

Exercises and techniques to manage stress and anxiety

ISBN: 978-1-84937-002-8, from www.uolearn.com
- ✓ Understand what stress is
- ✓ Become proactive in managing your stress
- ✓ How to become more positive about your life
- ✓ An easy 4 step model to lasting change

Studying for your Future

Skills for life, whilst you study

ISBN: 978-1-84937-047-9, Order at www.uolearn.com

✓ A checklist to put together a portfolio to show a prospective employer
✓ Learn the skills to prepare you for your degree
✓ Help you with literature reviews and writing skills
✓ Goal setting to help you focus on your future
✓ Sort out your time planning
✓ Improve your study skills and exam preparation
✓ Prepare for employment

How to Start a Business as a Private Tutor

ISBN 978-1-84937-029-5, from www.uolearn.com

This book, by a Lancashire based author, shows you how to set up your own business as a tutor.

✓ Packed with tips and stories
✓ How to get started - what to do and buy
✓ How to attract clients and advertise
✓ Free printable forms, ready to use
✓ Advice on preparing students for exams

Dreaming Yourself Aware

Exercises to interpret your dreams

ISBN: 978-1-84937-055-4, Order at www.uolearn.com

✓ Learn how to remember and record your dreams
✓ Structured approach to understand your dreams
✓ A large variety of techniques for dream interpretation
✓ Step by step instructions and worked examples
✓ Exercises to help you to find answers to problems
✓ Understand your motivation and reveal your goals
✓ Make positive changes to your life

Dreaming yourself aware gives a step by step guide to interpreting your dreams.

Coaching Skills Training Course

Business and life coaching techniques for

ISBN: 978-1-84937-019-6, from www.uolearn.com
- ✓ An easy to follow 5 step model
- ✓ Learn to both self-coach and coach others
- ✓ Over 25 ready to use ideas
- ✓ Goal setting tools to help achieve ambitions

A toolbox of ideas to help you become a great coach.

Successful Minute Taking

How to prepare, write and organise agendas and minutes of meetings

ISBN 978-1-84937-040-0, from www.uolearn.com

- ✓ Becoming more confident in your role
- ✓ A checklist of what to do
- ✓ Learn what to include in minutes

Learn to be an excellent meeting secretary.

Practical and Effective Performance Management

ISBN: 978-1-84937-037-0, from www.uolearn.com
- ✓ Five key ideas to understanding performance
- ✓ A clear four step model
- ✓ Key what works research that is practical
- ✓ A large, wide ranging choice of tools
- ✓ Practical exercises and action planning for managers

A toolbox of ideas to help you become a better leader.

Speed Writing

ISBN 978-1-84937-011-0, from www.uolearn.com
Easy exercises to learn faster writing in just 6 hours.

- ✓ "The principles are very easy to follow, and I am already using it to take notes."
- ✓ "I will use this system all the time."
- ✓ "Your system is so easy to learn and use."

"Don't live down to expectations.
Go out there and do something remarkable."
Wendy Wasserstein

Lightning Source UK Ltd.
Milton Keynes UK
UKOW04f1047081016

284772UK00008B/104/P